Investing 101:

How to start building wealth today

Franklin Fisher

Table of Contents

Chapter 1

Introduction

A. Importance of Investing

1. **Building Financial Security**
   Investing is crucial for building financial security. By putting your money into investments, you create the potential for your money to grow over time, rather than just sitting in a savings account earning minimal interest. This growth can help you achieve financial goals such as buying a home, funding education, or enjoying a comfortable retirement.

2. **Growing Wealth Over Time**
   Investing allows you to take advantage of the power of compounding, where the returns on your investments generate their own returns. This can lead to exponential growth of your wealth over time, significantly increasing your financial resources compared to saving alone.

B. Common Myths About Investing

1. **Investing is Only for the Wealthy**
   A common misconception is that investing is only accessible to those with a lot of money. In reality, many investment options are available for all financial levels. With the advent of online brokers and robo-advisors, you can start investing with small amounts of money, making it accessible to nearly everyone.

2. **Investing is Too Risky**
   Another prevalent myth is that investing is inherently too risky. While all investments carry some level of risk, the key is to understand and manage that risk appropriately. Diversification, research, and a long-term perspective can mitigate many of the risks associated with investing.

C. Purpose of the Guide

1. **Empower Beginners with Knowledge**
   This guide aims to empower beginners by providing essential knowledge about investing. Understanding the basics will help you make informed decisions and

build confidence as you start your investment journey.

2. **Provide a Step-by-Step Approach**
   To make the process less daunting, this guide offers a clear, step-by-step approach to investing. From setting financial goals to choosing the right investments, each section is designed to guide you through the process systematically, ensuring you can start building wealth today.

Chapter 2

Understanding the Basics of Investing

A. What is Investing?

1. **Definition and Key Concepts**
   Investing involves allocating money into various financial instruments or assets with the expectation of generating a profit or income over time. Key concepts include understanding the nature of assets, returns, and the time value of money.

2. **Difference Between Saving and Investing**
   Saving typically involves putting money aside in a secure, easily accessible place like a savings account, where it earns minimal interest. Investing, on the other hand, involves purchasing assets with the potential for higher returns, albeit with higher risk.

B. Types of Investments

1. **Stocks**
   Stocks represent ownership in a company. When you buy stocks, you become a shareholder and can benefit from the company's growth through dividends and capital appreciation.

2. **Bonds**
   Bonds are debt securities issued by corporations or governments. When you purchase a bond, you are lending money to the issuer in exchange for periodic interest payments and the return of the bond's face value at maturity.

3. **Mutual Funds**
   Mutual funds pool money from multiple investors to purchase a diversified portfolio of stocks, bonds, or other securities. They provide diversification and professional management.

4. **Exchange-Traded Funds (ETFs)**
   ETFs are similar to mutual funds but trade on stock exchanges like individual stocks. They offer diversification and typically lower fees.

5. **Real Estate**
   Investing in real estate involves

purchasing property to generate rental income or to sell at a higher price in the future. This can include residential, commercial, or industrial properties.

6. **Other Alternatives (e.g., Commodities, Cryptocurrencies)**
Alternative investments like commodities (e.g., gold, oil) and cryptocurrencies (e.g., Bitcoin) offer diversification and potential high returns but also come with higher volatility and risk.

C. Risk and Return

1. **Understanding Risk**
Risk in investing refers to the potential for losing money. Different investments carry different levels of risk, and understanding these risks is crucial for making informed decisions.

2. **Risk Tolerance and Personal Risk Profile**
Your risk tolerance is your ability and willingness to endure market fluctuations. It depends on factors like your financial situation, investment goals, and time horizon.

3. **Relationship Between Risk and Return**

 Generally, the potential for higher returns comes with higher risk. Balancing risk and return according to your risk tolerance and investment objectives is key to a successful investment strategy.

Chapter 3

Preparing to Invest

A. Setting Financial Goals

1. **Short-Term vs. Long-Term Goals**
   Financial goals can be broadly categorized into short-term and long-term objectives. Short-term goals typically span one to five years and may include saving for a vacation, a down payment on a car, or an emergency fund. Long-term goals, on the other hand, extend beyond five years and often involve major life events such as buying a home, funding a child's education, or retirement planning. Clearly distinguishing between these goals helps determine the appropriate investment strategies and time horizons for each.

2. **Importance of Clear Objectives**
   Establishing clear financial objectives is crucial for creating a focused investment plan. Clear goals provide direction and purpose, helping you stay motivated and

disciplined in your investment journey. They also allow you to measure progress and make necessary adjustments along the way. When setting goals, ensure they are Specific, Measurable, Achievable, Relevant, and Time-bound (SMART) to maximize their effectiveness.

B. Building an Emergency Fund

1. **Definition and Purpose**
   An emergency fund is a financial safety net designed to cover unexpected expenses such as medical emergencies, car repairs, or sudden job loss. The primary purpose of an emergency fund is to provide liquidity and financial stability during unforeseen circumstances, preventing the need to liquidate investments or incur high-interest debt.

2. **Recommended Amount**
   Financial experts generally recommend maintaining an emergency fund that covers three to six months' worth of living expenses. The exact amount can vary based on individual circumstances, such as job stability, income variability, and personal comfort levels. Keeping

these funds in a readily accessible account, like a savings account or money market account, ensures they are available when needed.

C. Managing Debt

1. **High-Interest vs. Low-Interest Debt**
   Effective debt management is a critical component of preparing to invest. High-interest debt, such as credit card balances and payday loans, can significantly erode your financial health due to the high cost of borrowing. Prioritizing the repayment of high-interest debt is essential as it typically outpaces potential investment returns. Low-interest debt, such as mortgages or student loans, may be more manageable and can be paid off over time while you also invest.

2. **Strategies for Paying Off Debt**
   There are several strategies to tackle debt efficiently:
   - **Debt Snowball Method:** Focus on paying off the smallest debts first while making minimum payments on larger debts. This approach

provides quick wins and boosts motivation.

o **Debt Avalanche Method:** Prioritize debts with the highest interest rates, which minimizes the total interest paid over time. This method can save more money in the long run.

o **Consolidation:** Combining multiple debts into a single loan with a lower interest rate can simplify repayment and reduce interest costs.

o **Automated Payments:** Setting up automatic payments ensures timely debt repayment, helping avoid late fees and penalties.

D. Budgeting and Saving

1. **Creating a Budget**
A well-structured budget is the foundation of financial planning. Begin by tracking all sources of income and categorizing expenses into fixed (e.g., rent, utilities) and variable (e.g., entertainment, dining out) categories. Analyze your spending patterns to identify areas

where you can cut back. Allocate a portion of your income to savings and investments, and adjust your budget as needed to align with your financial goals.

2. **Identifying Areas to Save** Finding ways to save money can increase the amount available for investing. Consider the following strategies:

   - **Reduce Discretionary Spending:** Cut back on non-essential expenses like dining out, subscription services, and impulse purchases.

   - **Shop Smart:** Look for discounts, use coupons, and compare prices to save on everyday purchases.

   - **Automate Savings:** Set up automatic transfers to your savings and investment accounts to ensure consistent contributions.

   - **Review and Adjust:** Regularly review your budget to identify new saving opportunities and ensure you are staying on track with your financial goals.

By setting clear financial goals, building an emergency fund, managing debt effectively, and creating a realistic budget, you can lay a strong foundation for successful investing and long-term wealth building.

Chapter 4

Getting Started with Investing

A. Choosing the Right Investment Account

1. **Brokerage Accounts**

   Brokerage accounts are versatile investment accounts that allow you to buy and sell a wide range of securities, including stocks, bonds, mutual funds, and ETFs. These accounts are not tax-advantaged, meaning any income or gains may be subject to taxes. However, they offer flexibility and access to a broad spectrum of investment options, making them suitable for both short-term and long-term investment strategies. When choosing a brokerage account, consider factors such as fees, account minimums, available investment options, and the quality of customer service.

2. **Retirement Accounts (IRA, 401(k), etc.)**

   Retirement accounts are designed to

help you save for retirement with tax advantages. The most common types include:

- **Individual Retirement Accounts (IRAs):** Traditional IRAs offer tax-deferred growth, meaning you pay taxes on withdrawals in retirement. Roth IRAs provide tax-free growth, allowing tax-free withdrawals in retirement, as contributions are made with after-tax dollars.
- **401(k) Plans:** These employer-sponsored plans allow you to contribute pre-tax income, reducing your taxable income for the year. Many employers offer matching contributions, effectively providing free money for your retirement savings. Roth 401(k) options are also available, offering tax-free withdrawals.
- **SEP IRAs and SIMPLE IRAs:** These accounts cater to self-employed individuals and small business owners, offering higher contribution

limits and tax benefits. When choosing a retirement account, consider factors such as contribution limits, tax treatment, and potential employer matches.

B. Selecting Investments

1. **Diversification and Asset Allocation**
   Diversification involves spreading your investments across different asset classes (e.g., stocks, bonds, real estate) to reduce risk. Asset allocation is the process of determining the optimal mix of asset classes based on your risk tolerance, financial goals, and time horizon. A well-diversified portfolio can help mitigate the impact of market volatility and improve the potential for long-term returns. Periodically review and rebalance your portfolio to maintain your desired asset allocation.

2. **Evaluating Investment Options**
   When selecting specific investments, consider factors such as:
   - **Risk Level:** Assess the risk associated with each investment and ensure it

aligns with your risk tolerance.

- o **Return Potential:** Evaluate the potential for growth or income generation.
- o **Time Horizon:** Match investments to your investment timeline. For example, stocks are typically better suited for long-term goals, while bonds may be more appropriate for shorter-term objectives.
- o **Fees and Expenses:** Be mindful of costs such as expense ratios, management fees, and trading commissions, as they can erode returns over time.
- o **Performance History:** While past performance is not indicative of future results, it can provide insight into how an investment has weathered different market conditions.

C. Using Investment Platforms

1. **Online   Brokers**

   Online brokers provide a platform for self-directed investors to trade securities and manage their portfolios. They offer a wide range of tools and resources, including research reports, educational content, and advanced trading features. When selecting an online broker, consider factors such as trading fees, account minimums, available investment options, and the quality of their trading platform.

2. **Robo-Advisors**

Robo-advisors use algorithms to create and manage a diversified portfolio based on your risk tolerance and financial goals. They offer low-cost, automated investment management, making them an attractive option for beginners and those looking for a hands-off approach. Most robo-advisors provide features such as automatic rebalancing, tax-loss harvesting, and personalized financial planning.

3. **Financial   Advisors**

Financial advisors offer personalized investment advice and portfolio management tailored to your specific needs and goals. They can help with comprehensive financial planning, including retirement planning, tax strategies, and estate planning. While financial advisors typically charge higher fees than robo-advisors, their expertise can be valuable for complex financial situations or investors who prefer a human touch. When choosing a financial advisor, consider their credentials, experience, fee structure, and whether they act as a fiduciary, meaning they are required to act in your best interest.

By choosing the right investment account, selecting appropriate investments, and utilizing suitable investment platforms, you can effectively start building and managing your investment portfolio. This structured approach ensures you are well-equipped to achieve your financial goals and build wealth over time.

Chapter 5

Developing an Investment Strategy

A. Long-Term vs. Short-Term Strategies

1. **Buy and Hold**
   The buy-and-hold strategy involves purchasing investments and holding them for an extended period, regardless of market fluctuations. This approach capitalizes on the long-term growth potential of markets, leveraging the power of compounding. It reduces the impact of short-term volatility and trading costs. Ideal for investors with long-term goals, such as retirement, this strategy requires patience and discipline to ride out market cycles without reacting impulsively to short-term market movements.

2. **Dollar-Cost Averaging**
   Dollar-cost averaging (DCA) is a strategy where you invest a fixed amount of money at regular intervals, regardless of the investment's price.

This approach mitigates the risk of investing a large sum at an inopportune time. By consistently investing, you buy more shares when prices are low and fewer when prices are high, potentially lowering your average cost per share over time. DCA is particularly useful for managing market volatility and maintaining a disciplined investment routine.

B. Rebalancing Your Portfolio

1. **Importance of Rebalancing**
   Rebalancing is the process of realigning your portfolio to maintain your desired asset allocation. Over time, market movements can cause your portfolio to drift from its original allocation, potentially increasing risk. Regular rebalancing ensures your portfolio remains aligned with your risk tolerance and investment goals, helping to manage risk and maintain diversification.

2. **How to Rebalance**
   To rebalance your portfolio, follow these steps:
   - **Review Your Asset Allocation:** Compare your

current portfolio allocation to your target allocation.

- o **Identify Overweight and Underweight Assets:** Determine which assets have grown beyond their target weights and which have fallen below.
- o **Sell and Buy Assets:** Sell a portion of the overweight assets and use the proceeds to buy more of the underweight assets, bringing your portfolio back to its target allocation.
- o **Frequency of Rebalancing:** Consider rebalancing annually or semi-annually, or when an asset class deviates by a certain percentage (e.g., 5-10%) from its target allocation.
- o **Cost Considerations:** Be mindful of transaction costs and tax implications when rebalancing, and try to minimize these expenses.

C. Staying Informed and Adjusting Strategies

1. **Keeping Up with Market Trends**
   Staying informed about market trends and economic developments helps you make better investment decisions. Regularly read financial news, follow market analysts, and review economic indicators to understand market dynamics. This knowledge can help you identify opportunities, manage risks, and adjust your investment strategy as needed.

2. **Adapting to Life Changes**
   Life changes, such as marriage, the birth of a child, career shifts, or approaching retirement, can significantly impact your financial goals and risk tolerance. Periodically review your investment strategy to ensure it aligns with your current circumstances and objectives. Adjust your portfolio as needed to reflect changes in your financial situation, time horizon, and investment goals.

By developing a comprehensive investment strategy that includes long-term and short-term approaches, regular rebalancing, and staying informed, you can effectively manage your portfolio and work towards achieving your financial goals. This proactive and disciplined approach helps you navigate market fluctuations and adapt to life changes, ensuring your investment strategy remains aligned with your evolving needs.

Chapter 6

Common Investment Mistakes to Avoid

A. Emotional Investing

1. **Panic Selling and Market Timing**
   Emotional investing often leads to panic selling during market downturns, which can lock in losses and hinder long-term growth. Attempting to time the market by buying low and selling high is extremely challenging and often results in poor performance. Emotional decisions driven by fear or greed can lead to selling investments at a loss during market dips and missing out on recovery gains. Maintaining a disciplined, long-term investment strategy helps avoid these pitfalls and takes advantage of market recoveries.

2. **Overconfidence**
   Overconfidence can lead investors to underestimate risks and overestimate their ability to predict market

movements. This may result in taking on excessive risk or concentrating investments in a few stocks or sectors. It's important to remain humble and realistic about your investing skills and knowledge. Relying on thorough research, diversification, and adherence to your investment plan can mitigate the risks associated with overconfidence.

B. Lack of Diversification

Failing to diversify your portfolio can expose you to unnecessary risk. Diversification involves spreading investments across various asset classes, sectors, and geographic regions to reduce the impact of any single investment's poor performance. A well-diversified portfolio can help smooth out returns and reduce volatility, protecting your investments from significant losses. Regularly review and adjust your portfolio to ensure it remains diversified and aligned with your risk tolerance and investment goals.

C. Ignoring Fees and Expenses

Fees and expenses can significantly erode investment returns over time. Common fees include expense ratios for mutual funds and

ETFs, trading commissions, and management fees for financial advisors. High fees can reduce the compounding effect on your investments, limiting long-term growth. To minimize the impact of fees, choose low-cost investment options, such as index funds and ETFs, and be mindful of transaction costs. Regularly review the fees associated with your investments and consider switching to lower-cost alternatives if appropriate.

D. Failing to Review and Adjust Investments

Investments should not be set on autopilot. Failing to regularly review and adjust your portfolio can lead to misalignment with your financial goals and risk tolerance. Market conditions, economic changes, and personal life events can all impact your investment strategy. Periodic reviews allow you to assess performance, rebalance your portfolio, and make necessary adjustments to stay on track. Establish a routine for reviewing your investments, such as quarterly or annually, and make adjustments as needed to ensure your portfolio remains well-positioned to achieve your financial objectives.

Chapter 7

Resources for Continued Learning

A. Books and Literature

1. **Recommended Reading List**
   - **"The Intelligent Investor" by Benjamin Graham:** A classic text on value investing that provides timeless wisdom on how to approach the stock market.
   - **"A Random Walk Down Wall Street" by Burton G. Malkiel:** This book covers various investment strategies and offers insights into the efficient market hypothesis.
   - **"Common Stocks and Uncommon Profits" by Philip Fisher:** Offers guidance on evaluating and selecting stocks based on qualitative criteria.
   - **"The Little Book of Common Sense Investing"**

by John C. Bogle: Advocates for low-cost index fund investing as a strategy for long-term success.

o **"Your Money or Your Life" by Vicki Robin and Joe Dominguez:** Focuses on financial independence and transforming your relationship with money.

o **"One Up On Wall Street" by Peter Lynch:** Shares insights from a successful fund manager on how to identify investment opportunities.

B. Online Courses and Tutorials

Numerous online platforms offer courses and tutorials on investing, suitable for all levels of experience. Some popular platforms

include:

• **Coursera:** Offers courses from top universities and institutions on various investment topics, including fundamentals of investing, financial markets, and portfolio management.

- **edX:** Provides access to courses on investing and finance from renowned institutions such as MIT, Harvard, and more.
- **Udemy:** Features a wide range of investment courses, from beginner to advanced levels, often with practical exercises and real-world applications.
- **Khan Academy:** Offers free tutorials on the basics of investing, personal finance, and economics, ideal for beginners.
- **Investopedia Academy:** Provides specialized courses on investing strategies, financial analysis, and trading, taught by industry experts.

C. Financial News and Websites

Staying informed about the latest market trends and economic developments is crucial for making informed investment decisions. Some reliable sources include:

- **Wall Street Journal (WSJ):** A leading source for financial news, market data, and economic analysis.
- **Bloomberg:** Provides comprehensive news coverage, market insights, and analysis on global financial markets.

- **CNBC:** Offers real-time market news, analysis, and investment advice, along with video content and interviews with industry experts.
- **Yahoo Finance:** Delivers up-to-date market news, financial data, and tools for tracking your investments.
- **Morningstar:** Provides in-depth research, analysis, and ratings on stocks, mutual funds, and ETFs.
- **Seeking Alpha:** A platform where investors share their analyses and opinions on various investment opportunities.

D. Professional Advice and Networking

Seeking professional advice and networking with other investors can provide valuable insights and support for your investment journey.

- **Financial Advisors:** Certified financial planners (CFPs) and other advisors can offer personalized investment advice and comprehensive financial planning based on your individual goals and risk tolerance.
- **Investment Clubs:** Joining an investment club allows you to learn

from and share ideas with other investors, providing a collaborative environment for discussing investment strategies and opportunities.

- **Professional Organizations:** Consider joining organizations such as the CFA Institute or the Financial Planning Association (FPA) for access to educational resources, professional development, and networking opportunities.
- **Conferences and Seminars:** Attend industry conferences, webinars, and seminars to stay updated on market trends, investment strategies, and emerging opportunities. These events also offer opportunities to network with industry professionals and other investors.
- **Online Forums and Communities:** Participate in online forums and communities, such as Reddit's r/investing or Bogleheads.org, where investors discuss strategies, share experiences, and offer support.

By leveraging these resources, you can continuously expand your knowledge, stay informed about market developments, and refine your investment strategies to achieve long-term financial success.

Chapter 8

Conclusion

A. Recap of Key Points

Throughout this guide, we've covered essential aspects of investing, including:

- Understanding the importance of investing for building financial security and growing wealth over time.
- Dispelling common myths about investing, such as the belief that it's only for the wealthy or too risky.
- Empowering beginners with knowledge and providing a step-by-step approach to starting their investment journey.
- Setting financial goals, building an emergency fund, managing debt, and budgeting effectively as prerequisites for investing.
- Choosing the right investment accounts, selecting investments, and using investment platforms to begin investing.
- Developing an investment strategy, including long-term vs. short-term

approaches, portfolio rebalancing, and staying informed.

- Avoiding common investment mistakes such as emotional investing, lack of diversification, ignoring fees, and failing to review investments.

B. Encouragement to Start Investing Today

Now that you have a solid foundation in investing principles and strategies, it's time to take action and start investing today. Remember, the earlier you begin investing, the more time your investments have to grow and compound. Even small contributions can make a significant difference over the long term. Don't let fear or uncertainty hold you back—take the first step towards financial empowerment and start building your wealth today.

C. Final Tips for Success in Investing

As you embark on your investment journey, keep the following tips in mind:

- **Stay Disciplined:** Stick to your investment plan and avoid making impulsive decisions based on short-term market fluctuations.

- **Diversify Your Portfolio:** Spread your investments across different asset classes and sectors to mitigate risk and maximize long-term returns.
- **Minimize Costs:** Be mindful of fees and expenses associated with your investments, and choose low-cost options whenever possible to maximize returns.
- **Stay Informed:** Continuously educate yourself about investing principles, market trends, and economic developments to make informed decisions.
- **Seek Professional Advice:** Consider consulting with a financial advisor or investment professional for personalized guidance and support.
- **Monitor and Review:** Regularly review your investment portfolio, assess performance, and make adjustments as needed to stay on track towards your financial goals.

With dedication, patience, and a sound investment strategy, you can achieve financial success and build a secure future for yourself and your loved ones. Start investing with confidence and watch your wealth grow over time.

Book description

"Investing 101: How to start building wealth today" is your essential roadmap to financial empowerment. Whether you're a novice investor or looking to enhance your investment knowledge, this comprehensive guide provides a step-by-step approach to building wealth and securing your financial future. Discover the importance of investing for long-term growth and learn how to dispel common myths that may be holding you back. From setting clear financial goals to choosing the right investment accounts and selecting suitable investments, this book covers all the essentials. Dive into practical strategies for managing debt, building an emergency fund, and creating a budget to support your investment journey. With insights on developing an effective investment strategy, avoiding common pitfalls, and accessing valuable resources for continued learning, "Unlock Your Wealth" equips you with the knowledge and confidence to start investing today. Take control of your financial destiny and unlock the door to a prosperous future with this empowering guide.

www.ingramcontent.com/pod-product-compliance
Lightning Source LLC
Chambersburg PA
CBHW070140230526
45472CB00004B/1616